The Humane Race,

The Human Erase,

and The Human

A Collection of Poems

Zach Bliss

Copyright © 2018 by Zach Bliss

All rights reserved. No part of this book may be replicated or transmitted on any form or by any means, electronic or mechanical; including photocopying without permission in writing from the Author.

ISBN: 978-0-9996208-4-7

The Humane Race, The Human Erase and The Human/Bliss- 1st ed.

1. Poems. 2. Poetry. 3. Verse.
4. Bliss 5. Social Commentary

NFB Publishing/Amelia Press
<<<>>>
119 Dorchester Road
Buffalo, New York 14213
For more information please visit
nfbpublishing.com

Contents

The Humane Race

Our History	9
King	10
Queen's Last Words	11
I Am Fodder	12
Ouroboros	14
Mr. Wayne, By The Joker	15
He Said To Man	16

The Human Erase

To The Now Last Man Alive	21
How Far Down	23
Life	24
Everlasting	25
Hollow	26
Breath	27
To No One	28

The Human

What About A Spark	33
Love	34
Foul Creation	35
Brick Wall Mouth	36
Inner Dialogue	37
Sucks	38
Palace Views	39
Choreographed	40
Pinocchio Said To God	43

The Humane Race

<u>Our History</u>

Committed baby species xenocide
Grew up to grieve our genocides
Still suicides destroy our lives
Homicidal still we scream and fight

We killed the Neanderthals

King

Face contorted,
The king extorted his morbid toll:
Stole from folks who can't afford it
And ordered sworn swords to silence souls.

A sworn servant of disservice,
The king forcefully averted memories of happy ways:
Redacting days
From the age when children smiled.

Reviled, as the child titled decider,
He decided to be wild while none the wiser.
Wide eyed and delirious,
The king consulted mysterious forces to steer him.

In his mind's eye wilds received him:
Believed him the righteous heathen
Whose sins are deeds needed.
So he did too.

He grew up greedy,
Blindly heeding grim whims and desires.
Without regard of the cost required,
The king longed and aspired to sit higher.

Wholly ignoring sordid tolls on his land,
Bloody sword in hand, the king warred and whored.
"Lord, I am holy. Act as I demand!"
His deranged command shrieked daily.

Prevailing and preordained,
The king's reign rained pain and daily perils
Upon a people who remained maimed,
Shamed by birth entirely.

Until, riled decidedly,
Mobs went wild finally:
Violently, with animosity,
Vied to commit just atrocities

And burned the king to death

<u>Queen's Last Words</u>

My Son,

No sooner than you were appointed then anointed
the only choice, the disjointed then adjoining masses
collapsed en masse upon us. They want us to
relinquish our inkling of hope: for the King to inhale
the smoke and ash of a past that left a lasting
impression upon them

And they've got him. Torched and pitchforked, those
I sent that sought to save him have been taken.
Tomorrow, we'll be witness to vicious and malicious visions
of wickedness: ill wills amassed upon a mass of men
descend again, ending us their means of rendering the
world their own.

Unknown to them, I'd trade the world away. All I'd require
in exchange for everything else is the time and space
to raise you. All my desires are to amaze you with what life
contains, and to praise you for what life you create.

They'll understand once I've said it. I'll plea and bray till
they get it. But tonight, I pray.

Goodnight,
My Love

I Am Fodder

I am fodder hear me soar
Around the world, surround the poor
Poor foddered people in tired steeples
Drained of all but rage unequaled

Ingrained in hate, abate unfeasible
Bullets fly blind through dirt shields wieldable
Wild bullets bite, blood flowers bloom
Blooms leave dirts dread red with gloom

Children grow in this crimson meadow
Grow into fathers foddered by metal venom
These fathers watch red meadow further
Then foddered fervors whisper of murders:

"Revenge against dread planting devils
Avenge red flowers planted forever
Loose metal serpents to feast on fodder
Loose metal fangs to sting their daughters "

Now preying grounds with slithering woe
Where peace did thrive so long ago
Lie both in hopeless dread read smoke
And hearts of those whose hearts have broke

For each foul strike that sinks to bone
Some heart is broke of one at home
Such dreadful break has no repair
Except to cause breakers despair

And now despaired is how I lie
A broken breaker sure to die
A feral father far from home
A flower of the field I've sown

I am fodder hear me roar
At futile fights forevermore
A bullet bites in brothers hearts
At lives that end before they start

Ouroboros

Dreary airs commandeered bold commoners
Despined
Space walks where their feet once whet
Rusty tomes mark their paths beaten to death
Broken homes hark that of theirs

Upon apocalypse
Spite incarnate breeds plight carnivorous
Man scurries to eat his own tail
Screaming war is hell through the flesh

<u>Mr Wayne, By The Joker</u>

No, I'm not insane
I'm not that different in the brain
I'm not indifferent to your pain
I'm on a mission, I'll explain:

A politician, Mr. Wayne
Apocalyptic and profane
His plot to pilfer, and to pain
My plight to hinder him, again

Again I'll wake to be his foe
And shake with fear that he should know
And paint a smile so nothing shows
My sickly guile disguises woes

And terrors Wayne has made me be
My errant ways and brave deceits
Despairing faces facing me
Deprived of futures truly free

No, I'm not insane
I'm not that different in the brain
I'm not indifferent to your pain
I know I'm laughing, I'll explain:

I've got to kill him, Mr. Wayne

He Said To Man

Oh children why, oh children woe
Oh children oh so long ago
Oh how you've grown, oh where you've gone
Oh what you've done

Some days ago, that's all it seems
Some days away is all I'd be
Some time alone, I thought you'd need
Sometimes I'm wrong

You spread the lies, you spread the woe
You say there's bounds my love should show
You call me god, and ask me why
But you should know

The Human Erase

<u>To The Now Last Man Alive</u>

You are the one who will carry on
Our ways our thoughts and who we are
Our space its gods they're truly yours
Through days and nights please do endure

Until your lonely dying breaths
Become humans' dying duress
Till brightening lightning lies at rest
Please carry on

Please live as long as time allows
As sparks that last from times that drowned
And memorial soul of what was lost
Alone you live to see us off

Our lives and token broken hearts
Our legends, fools, and sacred starts
Our skies, seas, and assorted views
The ways we often thought were true

Every love we ever had
Each treasured thing we clutched in hand
Each land we fought and died to save
And died on still till silence craved

All rust and dust and burning fires
That time sunk down and doused and sired

And now I sink and leave you last
Alone to live our last collapse
A lone anachronistic fool
Whose past is all he ever knew

And know it's all there ever was
And ever will and that's because
What lasts of who our species was
Is you

How Far Down

How far
Are we
Along
This path
Of dirt
And light-
Ning bolts?

Where dark
Dies bright
Dries tears
Of night
In homes
Those hol-
Lowd hearts

I live
A line
A life
Alive
A time
That time
Shall sink

And down
It goes
Our path
Our woes
You know
We know

The way

Life

Life is a series of fools
Who all run in circles in twos
If someone goes running in squares
Life cuts off their corners in pairs

There's a pair of stairs that goes up but not down
Those stairs are called life and you climb or you drown
Despair if you care to but sing if you don't
Know ever and ever don't care if you won't

If life could fathom, what might emerge on its breath?
Perhaps:
"Why must I submit to death?"
Death might answer:
"Silly series of fools. If life didn't drown, what else would it do?"
Then fire may claim:
"Not live, surely. Life upon life always leads to yours truly"

Everlasting

Though we burn it, life will outlast us
Its smoke leaves us choking on ash
As the ashes layer the flayer sings his prayer
Burying time's dagger deeper in man's ichor

Deeper still until collective will questions:
"We drowning people, what of us dreamers and seekers and sheeple?
Our legend is a scorn earthen body:
Sore scars lacing a pathetically apathetic pathology.

And no one will see it.
None will understand our broken earth secret.
No be'rs will wonder why the Sphinx has no nose,
Fewer souls still will study the ashes of prose."

Suppose an answer:
Blatant conflagration of all nations
As temporal flames maim all society
Eventually quietly man writhes
While eonic plagues claim memories remaining

But life dies never
Forever unsevered, life's strand wanders towards light immortal
While time twines towards future times near primordial

Hollow

My skin! It sags!
It crackles! It's rags!
My flesh!
My flesh!
O! Where is my flesh?

Flaking!
It's flaking!
I touched it!
Degrading!
I see it!
I see it!
My skin hid a secret!

I'm bone

Breath

When eyes
Do cry
Do try
To fly
Away
From what
They've seen

Then time
Has needs
To breed
And breathe
And breath

Can kill

<u>To No One</u>

I do not think I can carry on
Oh gods of men why have you gone

I'm so alone
I'm all I've got
It's not enough
I'd rather rot

I've traveled far
I've traveled near
I've seen it all
So crystal clear

The things we lost
What once was dear
The lands we took from those we feared
The lives we lost to cold's embrace
The lives we took from every place

Manifest and broken hearts
Our destiny as broken parts
Our empires and cities large
From dust to dust I saw the charge

Now brightening lightning strikes are scant
And trodden dirts where we did plant
Ourselves and our assorted ways
Decay and face their final days

We sowed our lot and so time came
To reap so now man's day's the same
As done and gone it's lost it's true
And now no one I scream to you

Alone I live to see us off
But I can't look
My will is lost

Please know I cannot carry on
Oh gods and men you're truly gone
So now I sink into the dark
Away from where we left no mark

The Human

<u>What About A Spark</u>

What about a spark does one most desire?
Maybe, to be consumed by ravish fire

Perhaps, the pleasure of spark extinguished
Cool dark drawn out warm light's relinquish

Darkness carries comforts, true
Knowledge no world may peek in you

But darkness costs a certain price
Brings lonely, whittled dreams of ice

And how cold can dreams of darkness be?
Before dark cold desires mark reality

So perhaps the desire is one of hunger
To live a world of heats, and lovers

To shine among bright endless spaces
Watch shadows dance from pleasant places

A hungry man once said
"Let there be light"
I wonder if he had his fill

Love

What greater love than sparking life?
Some child born through lovers strife
Trials borne, life sacrificed
So new life may love as well

<u>Foul Creation</u>

Oh Foul Creation! Why do I desire you?
Is the reason the same as why I aspire to
rise higher than is required of me? The
same reason I grow so tired and full of ire
when I'm finally offered opportunity? Oh,
Foul Creation! What did you do to me?

Brick Wall Mouth

Clashing against molars mortared
Verbal clubs leave them dentless

Languishing alone in spit
I hear your whispering hopes
Blow through teethen cracks

Beautiful reinvigoration
Then wretched desperation
Brew storms on ocean tongue

Swells become unweatherable
Mortar crumbles, timbre booms
Foundations scream away

Inner Dialogue

The mind said to the body:
"Oh my ever diminishing vessel!
Why can't you do all I demand?"
And the body said to the mind:
"Oh my temporary Lord!
Why demand of me what I cannot do?"

And the heart said to both:
"Oh my perpetual prisoners!
Because I own you."
Then continued:
"Mind, you can't do what I'm unwilling to
And body you'd die
If you tried to do what I'm unable.
You're both mine."

Then, finally aligned, the self said:
"Oh my suffering constituents!
You say our heart holds you prisoner,
But know this: it's also the key.
Our heart beats the cipher
That deciphers its own twisted alleyways,
Just listen."

<u>Suck</u>

O vampire of forgiveness!
Why won't you suck gently?
You've left me so blistered
What am I giving for?

Palace Views

Palace views cast warm shadows

On brisk death by cold.

Why? They shade

Why are you cold? It's not so bad

Things are ok in the end it's not

That bad

Shades say as they stand inside

On top of the world

Close to the sun

<u>Choreographed</u>

It's a worrisome game we two live
here and play, me and the dancing
man on the ceiling. I lie ill in my
bed, he looks down above head,
and neither of us say a thing.

I pretend he's not there, and he
pretends he's nowhere, as we
writhe in this restless medley.
Constantly dancing, sometimes
ceaselessly prancing, the man
is always as solemn as me.

We did this night after night, we
paired here in this plight, me and
the dancing man on the ceiling.
We lived true to our silence, a
world undisturbed to divide us, till
the night he descended on me.

He waltzed wanton upon me, then
want for breath struck me strongly,
as his grasp masked my neck gracefully.
He squeezed and he strangled, as I
dangled and dangled, off the
edge of sure finity.

Then I fell and I fell, through fell
skies and dry hells, as the
dancing man still strangled me.
Spots grew in my vision, and the
man said "Now listen,
as I tell you what happens to thee"

"I'm going to mangle your soul,
 I'll make you dream to be whole",
the dancing man whispered to me.
"I'm going to make you my slave,
then I'll dance on your grave!" The
strangling man shrieked out with glee

Then

Growing silent and somber,
filled with fury no longer, his eyes
pondered sonderously. He leaned
down and he kissed me, said
"Twas a pleasure dancing with
thee", and I saw my eyes no more
did see.

As he danced off to the distance, he
yelled back that he'd miss us,
and I realized the dancing man was
me.

Pinocchio Said To God

A ways away awaiting me
A day you'd say should never be
Delay it may but still to be
Delay I may but still I'll be

Someday I'll lay awake and kneel
And taste the sky and smell a field
Be real be real
To touch to feel
To hear to hurt to harm to heal
A boy a boy

A boy I'll be
The world I'll know
The love I'll see
The ways I'll grow
The tears the glee
A boy a boy
I'll be

www.ingramcontent.com/pod-product-compliance
Lightning Source LLC
Chambersburg PA
CBHW072041060426
42449CB00010BA/2390